Genre Realistic Fic

Essential Question
In what ways do people show they care about each other?

The Perfect Present

by Bronwen Wall

illustrated by Caroline Hu

Chapter 1
The Invitation

"Maggie O'Brien? What are you doing here?" Maggie swung around at the sound of her name. Her best friend, Tiva, stood in front of her with her hands on her hips and a grin plastered across her face.

"Hi, Tiva!" Maggie exclaimed and rushed to greet her friend. "Well, you know how much I love Irish dancing?"

Tiva smiled and nodded.

"This is where I have my lesson every Tuesday," Maggie said, waving at the Academy of Music and Dance building in front of them. "Now I'm waiting for Hunter to finish band practice and give me a ride home."

Maggie explained that her older brother, Hunter, and his Irish band practiced in a studio at the academy.

"Hopefully, I won't have to wait too long," Maggie said. "They're supposed to finish at 4:30, but they're always late. Anyway, what are you doing here?"

Maggie didn't think Tiva would have time for dancing. She spent most days after school playing baseball or basketball—depending on the season, of course.

Tiva shrugged and explained that her mom wanted her to take ballet. "She thinks it will improve my balance and coordination."

Maggie shook her head. That was hard to believe. Maggie had spent lots of time playing sports with Tiva and watching her shoot hoops. She knew that her friend was already really coordinated. On the court, she was a machine.

Tiva seemed to read her mind. "I know!" she exclaimed. "Try telling my mom, though. I had my first lesson today. I know you have to practice if you want to do well, but Mrs. Kent is so fussy." Tiva described how she spent most of the lesson practicing one small hand movement.

"I want to see you all dancing like graceful swans!" Tiva mimicked Mrs. Kent, then spoke in her regular voice. "Who wants to be a swan? I just want to leap around to some music that's got a beat!"

Maggie laughed and suggested that if Tiva tried Irish dancing, she could jump and whirl all around the place.

"Sounds more like my kind of dancing," Tiva said wistfully. "I'd love to try it one day."

A car horn tooted, and Tiva's mom pulled up to the curb. At the same time, Maggie heard Hunter's voice. She swung around to see him striding toward her.

The friends said good-bye, and Tiva walked over to where her mom was parked. She stopped at the car door and turned back to Maggie.

"Oh, I just remembered," she said. "I'm having my birthday party in a couple of weeks. I'll give you an invitation tomorrow. I hope you can come!" She grinned and got in the car.

Chapter 2
What to Give Tiva?

Maggie felt excited. Tiva's family had great parties with lots of games and fantastic food. Maggie had almost two weeks to find the perfect present.

Tiva was her best friend. Maggie wanted to give her a really special birthday present that would express exactly how important their friendship was to her. She wanted to give Tiva something unique, something that no one else could give her. But what?

Maggie was silent in the car on the way home, lost in her thoughts. She was so quiet that finally Hunter asked, "What's up, Mags?"

Maggie explained about Tiva's birthday present.

"Something she'd *really* like, huh?" Hunter thought for a moment. "How about some music?"

"No," Maggie replied. She'd already thought of music, and somehow that didn't seem special enough. Anyone could give Tiva some music.

"I could help you record some music," Hunter suggested. He explained that he could record her singing on his computer and then copy the songs onto an mp3 player. Hunter was excited about using the new music software on his computer.

Maggie shook her head and reminded her brother how bad she was at singing.

"Haven't you ever heard me singing in the shower?" she asked. "Dad says I screech like a rusty gate." They were both still laughing as Hunter swung the car into their driveway.

Hunter had given Maggie an idea. She could make Tiva a special birthday card. She found her mom in the kitchen and asked if she could print out some photos of herself and Tiva from the computer.

"Sure. What are you going to do with them?" her mom asked. Maggie explained about the birthday card and wanting to make something really personal. She remembered that her dad had taken some nice portraits of Tiva last summer, when the two families had gone to the lake together on vacation.

"Good thinking, Maggie," her mom said approvingly. "You've got an hour to work on it before dinner."

Maggie continued working on her card after school the next day. She had printed seven photographs. Some of them showed her and Tiva standing together in funny poses, and one showed Tiva holding an award the year she was Most Improved Basketball Player in the League.

All of the photographs made Maggie smile with happy memories.

Now she cut some of the photographs into shapes and arranged them all to fit on a piece of card stock. She drew stars on with her colored pens and added a birthday greeting. Then she used her glue stick on the empty spaces on the card and sprinkled glitter all over the top.

By the time Maggie had finished, her card looked fantastic and sparkled like a star.

Hunter walked past just as Maggie finished. He gave a low whistle. "Whew! Nice going. Who knew we had the Picasso of birthday cards in our midst? Maybe you can't sing that well, but you sure can dance and make great cards!"

Maggie smiled. She appreciated the compliment, and it gave her yet another idea.

She turned to her brother with a broad grin on her face.

"What?" he asked, suspicious now. "What do you want?"

Maggie shook her head. "Oh, nothing. You've just given me another idea, that's all," she said mysteriously. "I've got to work on it some more, but I just might take you up on your offer to help me!"

The next day after school, Maggie drew up a plan for Tiva's present. It might work, but was she really skilled enough to do it? And would Tiva like it? It was time to ask her mom.

Chapter 3
A Great Idea

Maggie's mom listened carefully while she explained her idea.

"So do you think I can do it?" Maggie finished nervously.

Her mom smiled and nodded. "I think giving her a dance lesson is a fantastic idea, Maggie, and there's no reason why you can't do it. You don't have much time to plan, though, so you're  going to need to get serious about organizing and practicing. I think you'll be great, and I'm sure Tiva will love it!"

Maggie's mom suggested that she make a written plan for the Irish dance lesson. Then she could call her teacher to make sure her plan would be good for a beginner.

Of course, she also needed to check with Hunter, because she was going to need his help for her plan to be successful.

Maggie spent the weekend planning her private dance lesson for Tiva. She thought about what she was taught when she started dancing. Then she thought about the kinds of things Tiva liked doing.

Hunter agreed when she asked if he and his band would play for her private lesson with Tiva.

"No problem, Mags," he said, and he offered to help her figure out what music to play for the lesson.

Maggie grinned. So far her plan was working out perfectly.

Now Maggie just had to draw the gift certificate for Tiva, offering her one free Irish dance lesson.

The lesson would take place during the practice time of the world-renowned Irish band Hunter O'Brien and His Friends. The instructor would be the well-known Irish dancer Maggie O'Brien! Markers, glue, and glitter flew across paper once more.

Maggie got up early on the morning of the party. Her mom helped her cut and arrange a bouquet of flowers from the garden for Tiva.

Maggie felt strangely nervous as she walked up the path to Tiva's house. She had already seen two other friends from school walking in, carrying large, colorfully wrapped presents. Maggie only held one slim envelope and the flowers.

She hummed one of the Irish tunes Hunter would play at their lesson and thought about the time she had spent with him selecting the right music. After all the work they'd put in, she really hoped Tiva would like her present.

When she saw Tiva, Maggie felt so nervous that she thrust the flowers and envelope at her friend and squeaked, "Happy birthday!"

After the cake, Tiva sat down to open presents. Maggie held her breath as she heard Tiva rip open the envelope. The silence seemed to last forever, then Tiva's arms encircled her.

"Oh, Maggie! That's so cool! An Irish dance lesson with you is the perfect present!"

Maggie was filled with emotion.

"Okay, everyone, follow me. It's time for some games!" Tiva exclaimed, and everyone streamed outside.

When the party was over, Tiva took Maggie upstairs to her room. "I can't wait for our dance lesson. I'm going to have to figure out what to do with all these!" Five new basketballs sat in a neat row along the wall.

"Besides, basketball is history," Tiva said with a laugh. "I'm totally into Irish dancing now!"

Respond to Reading

Summarize

Use the most important details from *The Perfect Present* to summarize the story. Your graphic organizer may help you.

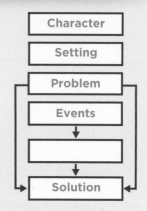

Text Evidence

1. How is *The Perfect Present* an example of realistic fiction? Use details from the story to explain. **GENRE**

2. What is Maggie's problem? How does she solve it? **PROBLEM AND SOLUTION**

3. What does the metaphor "she was a machine" mean on page 3? **SIMILES AND METAPHORS**

4. Write about the steps Maggie took to prepare her present for Tiva. **WRITE ABOUT READING**

Compare Texts
Read about how a boy shows he cares about his grandfather.

Fly Me to the Moon

Toby sat in the back of the car with a face like thunder. He couldn't believe it. His parents wouldn't let him bring his game Space Adventures on the visit to Poppa at the nursing home. He'd almost gotten his space shuttle to the next level. Now he'd have to start the whole level again.

Things didn't improve when they arrived at the nursing home. "Would you like a cup of tea, Poppa?" Toby's mom asked.

Poppa just grunted.

"Great!" Toby's dad whispered to his mom. "Another grumpy bear."

Toby glowered.

"We should leave these two to grumble together," his dad whispered again.

"Good idea. We'll get that tea, Poppa," Toby's mom said, and his parents left the room.

Poppa sighed. "I'm feeling old, Toby." He dragged a large box from under his bed and laid it on the table. The box was full of tiny airplane parts.

"It's a model of a Tiger Moth," Poppa explained, "but I'm too shaky to put it together properly. My eyes aren't sharp enough either."

Toby studied the pieces. He could see a strut that would slot in to support a wing.

"Maybe I could help," he suggested. Poppa smiled for the first time that morning. Toby smiled back.

They worked together for the next half hour, and Poppa described the model planes that he'd started collecting 40 years ago. He even had some of the first model spaceships. Toby gasped. Suddenly he was telling Poppa all about Space Adventures. Poppa listened closely.

"So when you reach the next level, which planet are you launched to?" Poppa asked.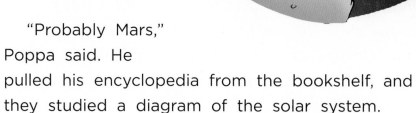

"I don't know."

"Probably Mars," Poppa said. He pulled his encyclopedia from the bookshelf, and they studied a diagram of the solar system.

Toby was fizzing with excitement in the car on the way home as he told his mom and dad about Poppa's model planes.

"Maybe I should bring Space Adventures with us next weekend so that Poppa can try it out," Toby suggested. "It will help him move his stiff fingers."

His mom laughed. "I think Poppa would like that, Toby. It could really take off."

Make Connections

How did Toby and his grandfather help each other? ESSENTIAL QUESTION

How do the characters in *The Perfect Present* and *Fly Me to the Moon* show they care about each other? TEXT TO TEXT

Focus on

Genre

Realistic Fiction Realistic fiction tells a story that could be true. Writers use believable characters and settings, and the plots usually involve the kinds of problems that many of us share. As readers we can identify with the characters and their problems almost as if we knew them ourselves.

Read and Find In *The Perfect Present*, Maggie's problem is finding the right birthday present. Does that seem believable to you?

In *Fly Me to the Moon*, Toby is more interested in his space game than visiting Poppa. Does that seem believable to you?

Your Turn

Compare yourself with one of the characters in either of the stories. Think about the ways you are similar and different. What is another problem the character might have to deal with? What would you do if you were in his or her position?

With a partner, discuss your characters and how they resolved the problems you gave them. Are your problems and solutions realistic?